Poetry by the Canal

An anthology of new poetry inspired by the Rochdale Canal in Littleborough from Rock Nook to Summit, and the history and natural history of the surrounding area.

First Published December 2023

Poetry by the Canal

ISBN: 978-1-914458-32-3
A catalogue record for this book
is available in the British Library

Selection and anthology design copyright 2023 Seamus Kelly
Poems copyright 2023 individual authors
Foreword copyright 2023 Roy McFarlane

Cover Photograph - (c) 2023, John Cannell,
Littleborough U3A Photography Group

Published by P2D Books Ltd

Printed and bound in England by P2D Books

The project organisers and participants wish
to express our thanks to:
Crook Hill Community Benefit Fund
for their sponsorship which has made this
publication possible.

The Canal & River Trust
for their support, and for introducing the Canal
Laureate, Roy McFarlane, and The Poetry
Society to this project.

We are also grateful to the
Friends of Hare Hill House,
who work to restore the park and house,
for welcoming us into their venue.

Foreword

The Rochdale Canal crossing the Pennines, known for its steep climb with lots of locks, provides the inspiration for Poetry by the Canal. Here, we find the power of poetry to gather, and lovingly evoke, the past and elicit into life the spirit of the people and the area, as we sail along the canal. This collection carries the weighty subjects of Empire, Industrial Revolution, the Summit tunnel fire and the making of khaki drill uniforms used for the First World War; and yet brings a microscopic insight into the lives of dragonflies.

There are laments for times past, love songs filled with the alliteration of local names, "Warland, Walsden, Lightowlers Lane." Historical events turned into mythical tales. Haikus everywhere, like 'Haiku at Rock Nook' by Sandra Buckley, and Ray Stearn's Ballad, 'Where the kingfisher, heron and otter now dwell', stories to be found amongst the ruins of a mill tower. Rook Nook Mill, the beating heart of the collection, "Another behemoth rising beside the canal."

These poets create an alchemy for the reader and the written words to be one in the experience of Rochdale Canal. From the navvies building the canal cutting deep into the land, to the commercialism and tourism of today. Often in times of uncertainty the poet comes to the forefront to remind us of being human and of the world around us in all its glory and frailties. Poetry by the Canal is heartfelt and full of splendour, hope and joy to behold.

Roy McFarlane FRSL
Canal Laureate England & Wales

Contents

The Rochdale Canal,

A dark satined ribbon curving, maternal,
protecting the town. Past derelict mills,
past homes and a warehouse.
Places with names that tell of their ancestry
Warland, Walsden, Lightowlers Lane.

Her banks are home to rat, to otter.
A pathway for badger, squirrel and fox.
Midges and butterflies dance on her surface.
Kestrel and Geese watch from above.
A hunting ground for the steel eyed Heron.
Camouflaged, still, shrouded in mist.

Her surface chokes with human detritus,
bottles, cans, half smoked fag- ends.
Plastic bags of mysterious objects,
a toddler's pushchair, a doll with no head.
Under her bridges, secrets are whispered.
She goes on her way telling no tales.

Clouds and rainbows reflect in her waters
wavelets caste diamonds over the weir
children lift arms, squealing their pleasure
Kingfishers flirting, Sparrows' darting,
anxious mothers, holding small hands
watching the ebb and flow of the water
learning the coming and going of life.

Eileen Earnshaw

Rock Nook

A fast-flowing stream bubbles over rocks,
racing down the hillsides, towards the canal.
Water to feed industry, and to feed the workers.
Another behemoth rising beside the canal.

Saws, chisels and ringing hammers cut stone,
shovels mix sloppy, sloshing mortar,
rivets and bolts fix the ironwork,
and boots stomp up and down ladders.

The scaffold, ladders and the banter come down,
and newly built looms are running,
ratter-tat-tat, ratter-tat-tat,
beside the canal.

Brand new khaki drill, woven, bagged, delivered,
fit for soldiers for heading to war,
to, one day face the
ratter-tat-tat of enemy guns, beside the Somme.

A monument to industrial innovation,
through cotton, glass fibres,
Aramid and Carbon,
beside the canal.

The weaving unwound, replaced,
by chattering knitting machines,
and yet more new fabrics.
All is changing, beside the canal.

Fire spat and crackled, beside the canal, in 2015.
Roofs gone, floors burnt, charred and fallen,
rocking the foundations of Rock Nook Mill,
monument to Littleborough past.

Brick and stone, solid and quiet for so long,
crack, crunch and crash to the ground,
men and machines must bring down the rest,
to a pile of stone, beside the canal.

The future is unsure.
The future is always unsure,
except for change, there is always change.
The fast-flowing stream bubbles over rocks,
racing down the hillside, towards the canal.

Seamus Kelly

The Mill

Bobbins spin and turn
Cotton dust hangs in the air
Eyes sting and hands yearn

Machinery groans
Hungry workers feed the thread
Weary to their bones

Nic Holliday

Haiku at Rock Nook

canalside deluge
parched soil replenishing
nature's rebalance

heron stands for hours
blending into rustling reeds
poise raised to an art

crumbling mill tower
rooks invade last wall standing
forlorn silhouette

moonlit bird of prey
feathered hunter flying low
nocturnal shimmer

Sandra Buckley

Haiku

Rolling big dark clouds
lit by pockets of sunlight
glinting on water.

Slimy wet wooden
fences along the canal
watching the water.

Christine Longhurst

The Bell Tolls

The bell tolls loudly
sadness fills the air.
The final shift is over
how will we survive?

Three generations redundant,
hunger the way ahead,
stealing to live.
A community destroyed

The future is a dark place.
Without hope we die.
Then why do politicians say
"We never had it so good."

Elizabeth White

Haiku

Yellow light shining
Canal reflecting
Moonlit algae

Elizabeth White

Rock Nook Relic

Under a grey, lowering sky,
an operation is taking place.
The area is marked, cordoned off.
Drilling, whirring, assails the ears.
A yellow army of tractors
is ripping out the belly of Rock Nook Mill.

One tower stands alone, erect: a dowager lady.
balustrade for a coronet.
A last remaining vestige of life.
Dull, occluded light is visible
through empty, sightless windows,
oblivious to the carnage of stone below.

Different layers of her life are on view.
Age darkens her lower facade
like lost memories.
Moments of lightness, brightness
highlight patches on upper sectors.
A portent of happier times?

A blocked up doorway. A mystery?
Is this where her secrets are hidden?
Straggling foliage, erupts, unkempt
from the tower's turret,
reminiscent of a balding, old head,
whose hair has thinned erratically through time.

The canal below, flows eternally onwards.
A mirrored pathway, reflecting demise.
Observer of Rock Nook Mill's history,
A testament to her working life.
Verdancy frames the canal banking beyond,
as life, impervious to mortality passes on.

Glenis Meeks

Ripples

Ripples and dappling light
in sunlit, silent beauty.

Ripples and dappling light.
Rainfall, spattered greyness.

A relic of bygone progress
created by labour of many,
living and toiling in poverty.
Desolate.

Travelling together
road, railway and canal
following roses of red and white,
rippling, dappling light.

Christine Longhurst

Where the kingfisher, heron, and otter now dwell

An audience is very rare today,
where the heron and otter and kingfisher dwell.
From the piles of rubble, no one could say,
where the heron and otter and kingfisher dwell.
That once a great mill occupied this space,
where the voices of looms kissed a granite face,
And mill workers had to know their place.
where the kingfisher, heron, and otter now dwell.

"Con Grandezza" as a frozen poem,
where the heron and otter and kingfisher dwell.
Never seen now, despite your knowing,
where the heron and otter and kingfisher dwell.
From on old O.S. map, staved loud and clear
this grand old mill stood here for many a year
and the mill workers lives were not held dear
where the kingfisher, heron, and otter now dwell.

Sit with your sandwich beside the canal.
Where the heron and otter and kingfisher dwell.
Imagine the sight, and the sound, and the smell,
where the heron and otter and kingfisher dwell.
Of a steam powered mill pouring out its grime,
where khaki drill marked out its time,
and the worker's clogged feet had to toe the line.
Where the kingfisher, heron, and otter now dwell.

Heron sings from her tree top nest,
where the heron and otter and kingfisher dwell.

Dog Otter chitters from the place he knows best.
where the heron and otter and kingfisher dwell.
While Kingfisher dives for fish, unseen.
And the audience? It's like they never have been.
Was nature's live opera only a dream?
Where the kingfisher, heron, and otter now dwell.

Ray Stearn

Rock Nook Mill

What have you seen
looking over the water,
looking over the railway and road?
The barges, the trains, the cars and the lorries,
traffic transporting their load.

What have you heard
sounding over the water
sounding over the road and the railway?
The school with its children,
their chatter and calling
echoing through their lives daily.

Things remain and some things change
as time passes on.
Looking over the water, the railway and road'
we see your sad ending -
a scar on the hillside,
watched by the water, the railway and road.

Christine Longhurst

Revolution

Machinery attacks the majestic beast.
Guts spill onto the ground.
Bricks tumble, unwanted,
Crumbling into dust.

The Pandora's box is prized open.
Two walls knitted together,
reveal splashes of pink, brown and blue.
Nature's new complexion.

Once-grey, windows are broken,
light swoops and swirls,
birds nest in young trees
sprouting in the gaps.

From its frail carcass
metal arms reach out,
and embrace a new age,
a new beginning.

Nic Holliday

Herons

Thomas said 'Herons, steeple-stemmed, bless'.
But my heron offers no benediction, she fishes,
for the souls of men long gone?
Consumed by the now-still mill?

Graham Haynes

Mills and Herons

Look at the mill, half gone.
Once it gave a purpose to the noise and dark toil
of the canal below,
its demise means a new peace will become the rule,
no jarring of the eye or of the soul.
Its past is forgotten, and its future will pass into memory.

Graham Haynes

Leaning on the lock gate

Late summer, the day is passed,
cliff and hill stand sentinel, the valley secure,
lock gate rough beneath the palm.

They come, the folk memories,
Irish voices, satin soft, scarred hands,
bent backs, a muted clang of shovel,
as veins of stone and prosperity grow.
A clatter of clogs, a laughter of children,
women, shawl wrapped with anxious eyes
helpless as illness takes its toll.

Past, present, distance entwine.
Bargees with rakish air, exotic accents
loading coal and fine-spun wool.
The horses, the barges moving majestic,
here today, gone tomorrow
leaving lovers, ignoring the sabbath
on the path, to far off Halifax.

Another time, another culture.
Here's the rollers, the pinnies,
the nylon headscarves. Shoes made in Taiwan,
dresses in India. The gentrification
of homes by the water.
Nature reclaims the land that was hers.

Here in the gentle globe of the evening,
Echoing sounds, the songs of the past.
A sacred hiatus, darkness comes calling
the place you were born sings in your bones.

Eileen Earnshaw

Rhiannon

She stands, statuesque,
alone in the field,
scarecrow like,
surveying the scene.

Patrolling the threshold,
guarding the sedges,
Rhiannon stands tall,
patiently waiting.

Elegant hunter,
gently pacing,
softly stepping, poised,
before spearing the water.

Sensing my presence,
crest ruffled by breeze,
she lunges forward,
wings unfurled, across the pound.

Chris O'Ryan

Lock 48

Cobbled sets stretch up and over the ancient bridge
facing Lock 48.
Heavy, black painted, wooden beams with rabbit tips
lie adjacent to the steep, stone embankment,
connecting to huge, weed encrusted, gates.
Iron machinery, cogs within cogs, convey mystery
to the ignorant onlooker, curious about its machinations,
unaware the key is an unwinding windlass.

Painted yellow cobbles set in lines
provide grip for straining feet
as the massive beams are manipulated, pushed
to release the constrained water.
Disengorging noisily, lustily, happily, it fills the lock,
lifting the gaudily painted, narrow boat upwards.
A time-tested feat, enacted throughout two centuries,
leaving memory markers, littering the towpaths.

Glenis Meeks

Haiku

Still water stands
Heron ponders
Treats below

Elizabeth White

Reflections

Vast open skies
Grey clouds loom above
reflecting in the canal's water.

Patchwork hills hug the canal
cut from Earth's cloth
Imagined, moulded, crafted

The canal reaches its long arm
to the Weavers in the mill.
Singing together, their songs
carry across to the Navvies
who join in with their songs of Green Emerald land.

Pain and hope are threaded together,
weft and warp.
Warp and weft.

Nic Holliday

Odonata Anisoptera

Once there was a creature,
nymph,
five years, more,
spent
in wet, gloom and murk,
occasional sunshine,
(After all this is Littleborough, and
this is the canal.)
Grew stronger, larger,
threw off skin fifteen times.
Until one warm morning
while Earth was still dark,
emerged from the murk,
crawled up a stem.
Waited.
While Sun warmed.

This time skin split in two,
head emerged, then thorax,
with effort like pumping iron.
Rested a while.
Kinetic energy, flowing molten steel, freed the abdomen,
while sun bathed it warm.
Creature grew, swelling, pumping fluid,
expanding in body and wings,
while the 30,000 facets of new eyes
observed a whole new world,
way above any earlier horizon.
Legs grip

but no longer walk.
So away creature flew,
testing out new wings,
two pairs.

Anisoptera, Anisoptera, Anisoptera.
Flying by day observing the world all around.
Flying strong,
hovering, hawking, darting
backwards, forwards,
swooping.
All four wings working
independently.
Legs now make a basket for prey
Which mandibles rip into, toothed, designed only to kill.
Odonata, Odonata, Odonata.
Voracious carnivore
in both lives.
No sting
to threaten most.
Beware of the terrifying name;
Dragonfly.

Ray Stearn

Empire Builders

They came from a place of deprivation
to one of exploitation.
These men left their kin and dug the way for
empire's stolen goods.
Rochdale Canal, one monument to rapacious revolution.
The railway came and slowly drained
your reason for existence.
Now it a place for leisure, boats decorated to ape the past,
draw cooing admiration from the towpath's dog walkers.

It is a ribbon for relaxation where once
there was dark toil.
Only the herons and the locks remain to punctuate the
solitude which has displaced
the loneliness of the bargees.
Gentle reflection sometimes conjures the raucous
exchanges, and this tranquil place once more
assumes its dark mantle.

Graham Haynes

Haiku

Swishing canal boats
hills, horses and llamas look
Summit's going on!

Dave Broome

Cottages

This poem is about the boarded-up cottages near lock 40:

Were the houses, now boarded,
once homes that were lived in?
Did they eavesdrop on family life?

Were the houses, now boarded,
the shelter of people?
Of children, of husband and wife?

The windows like eyes looking over Lock 40
their dark sockets still remain.

The doors were openings,
which closed on the world,
shutting in problems and pain.

Christine Longhurst

Haiku

Floating, still, in a gentle breeze,
Water, coloured with the leaves:
Autumn's windfall from the trees.

Chris Spankie

Bessie

Dawn is breaking
Nature awakes
The lock beckons
The boat prepares

Eyes tired and heavy
Baby at her breast
Bessie watches
The boat rise

Five lively children
Permanently hungry
Tears flow
The boat stops

The lock is full
Paddle released
Gates opened
The boat moves

Day is ending
The horse is fed
Children escape
The boat sleeps

Elizabeth White

The Towpath Leads . . .

The towpath leads to the Summit Inn
where, on opening the tunnel,
investors gathered in celebration;
where weary weavers, heading home,
could climb aboard the 19 tram;
where charabancs, filled on summer Sundays
with flat-capped fellows and cloche-hatted girls,
left for the coast or Hollingworth Lake .

The towpath leads to lapwing in flight,
peewit whistle calling, calling,
riding the winds like a crazy kite;
to black-dotted fields of jackdaw and crow;
to Canada geese stalking the path,
hissing, spitting as walkers pass.

The towpath leads to dark lock gates
where massive timbers hold a level,
wearing away, leaking in places,
spouts of water spurting in corners,
shlushing and splashing out of the sluice
dispersing the leaves, autumn's confetti.

The towpath leads to Rock Nook mill,
first producer of khaki drill,
where marching proud in his uniform,
Edwin Chadwick, aged eighteen,
left his loom to go to the Somme. . . .
Now all that stands is an empty shell.

Chris O'Ryan

Holly, Oak and Yule

For aeons the calendar of the Sun maintained peace between the sparring Kings. At the Winter Solstice on December 21st the biannual exchange would take place, when waxing Oak would regain the throne, and the days would begin their gradual growth, until midsummer, when Holly would once more take on the wheel of the seasons.

On 20th December 1984 a calamitous event took place when a freight train of petrol tankers was derailed in the Summit tunnel. The fire that erupted was of such Sun flaming ferocity that the soil was warmed to the point of plants preparing to emerge 3 months ahead of their scheduled arrival. Nature's precarious balance was placed in jeopardy, and even risked the outbreak of war between the two Kings. This could have acted as a further portent of the part Human activity played in global warming. The following is an imagining of the exchange between the Holly king and the Oak king.

What trickery is this to undermine my rule? Does my brother take me for a fool?

I'm not yet halfway through my reign. I know who stands the most to gain.

Dare you accelerate the fight between my darkness and your light?

A fiery pillar rose 40 metres and drove a burning wedge between us.

The smoke that followed the furnace's flare did not the harm of your slight repair.

The turn is due when your light will shine, but until then the dark is mine.

The earth has warmed before the Spring. Who else but you wants such a thing?

22

Dear brother be not so malcontent.
I swear it was an accident.
A mortal man made a mistake.
Pray don't harangue me in its wake.
The effects of Man we're yet to see
that place the world in jeopardy.
Until their actions change the weather
it's best that we two stick together,
in the hope our brotherly harmony's
enough to keep Earth's mercury climb to
1.5 degrees.

Chris Spankie

Tunnel entrance:

Autumn colours sit
astride the railway snaking
into the dark mouth.

Christine Longhurst

Unlikely

Small movement, a twitching,
fast flutter of wings,
dark shape bobs up and down.

A white-throated bird
diving into a ditch, then
flies up to the stony weir.

Submerged in the flow,
clamping on to the setts,
ready to pounce for a catch.

A dipper - a song bird
of wild creeks and glens,
of forest streams dappled in shade.

An unlikely sight
this bird of the wild,
foraging by the canal.

But nature is changing,
and so are the birds,
in their struggle to survive.

Seeking green spaces
alongside clean water,
venturing out to explore.

Building a new life
by the stagnant canal –
an unlikely spot for sure!

Just as the first sighting
of a herd of alpacas
grazing up Summit above the canal.

An unlikely addition,
at one time unheard of,
but nowadays fitting right in.

Sandra Buckley

Dance of Cruelty

'Oh, how beautiful', we cry as we spot the hawk,
hoping to see the perpendicular descent.
Never acknowledging the terror in the rodent's eyes,
the final beatings of the imploring heart.

For her, tiny mouse, the cruel dance is performed daily.
Above, the shadow hovers to a poignant standstill,
sucking the light away.
This is death, but when will it come?

Graham Haynes

The Magnet

Like iron filings to a magnet.
Walkers are drawn to explore the Rochdale,
as it winds through the lower Pennines.
Coming by rail, tram and bus,
assisted by a GMT pass,
following one of many threads,
weaving through our history.

Their eyes alight with pleasure,
reliving the segments of their journeys.
Manchester to Rochdale,
Rochdale to Littleborough,
Littleborough to Todmorden,
Todmorden to Hebden,
Hebden Bridge to Sowerby Bridge,
the Yorkshire names slipping from their Lancashire
tongues,
like butter off a spoon.

Echoing those rebellious ramblers before them,
these walkers escape the Urban Sprawl,
though, unlike on Kinder Scout, they are welcomed here,
finding peace and tranquillity in this place,
where nature reclaims a declining industrial landscape.

Marilyn Aldred

The Cut

Splitting earth in six foot drifts,
shifting soil to the height of men.
Toiling above others' heads, below their boots
jump down and dig again.

Stacked three men deep, slaving,
crushed, weary of God's sweetest earth.
The dark lock grows, swallows all hope
I have become far less than I am worth.

Unrelenting hand drives rough shovel,
swings pick high to claim fresh ground.
Darkness sends me to my hovel,
your tender comfort never found.

Five men deep now, inching forward,
thirty feet below the first cruel cut.
Filthy, lost and far from my heart's home,
I return, shackled, to the navvies' hut.

Maggie Kelly

Defiant in the darkness

"This tunnel will defy the rage of tempest, fire, war or wasting age."
Thomas Longridge Gooch, tunnel designer.

Do they linger still,
shovels and picks
ringing into the night?

Are they spaced at regular intervals,
one every 70 yards,
or are they clustered
in shared death, as shared work?

Measuring the value of labour is easy,
measuring value of lost lives, less so.
So when our train rattles through the darkness,
do they still feel its passing,
and do we feel theirs,
every four seconds?

Seamus Kelly

O'er t'brush.

You looked the other way as
the poisoned earth destroyed our lives.
As our little ones died of starvation.
Earth to earth, where were you?
Where were you?
The priest, your servant pointed our way
to this hell on earth.
Did you not look down on us,
as we carried out our dead,
only to bury them in the soil
they had dug by the light of a tallow.

Forgive me Lord.
For I am only a man who needs the comfort of a woman.
Please don't condemn me now,
as I jump the broom with Sarah Anne.
Turn away now, as I lead her to the hovel,
I built from sods from the tunnel,
that monstrous hole,
where I labour from dawn till dusk,
never seeing the light of day.

Do you hear me now Lord, as I pray,
for my darlin' Bridie and my bairns waiting for me,
back home in County Mayo?

Marilyn Aldred

41 Souls

"Defy the rage of tempest, war and wasting age",
laying the first brick, Dickinson said without sweat.
Glib proclamations spoken in a suit and waged,
cementing the gap between rich and poor..and yet,
deep in this hillside, tunnelling is gut wrenching,
a cost to link up cities from Lancs and Yorkshire.
3 years toil, fear and injuries still stenching,
this Summit Tunnel reaching across the border.

1 quarter of a million the cost….or more?
Millions of bricks, 6 layers deep, keeping it
safe from collapse from ravage fire in '84.
Built by a 1000 of us everyday 'brickin it'.

My name you know not, yet this was the cost,
for I was 1 of the wasted souls lost.

Dave Broome

Summit Tunnel Fire, 1984

Explosion, fire and blinding light,
made the national news!
Destruction of that route into the future?
No, not quite.

Before the trains came back
we walked through there along the tracks,
our footprints in the mud and stones,
still there, or mingled with those long gone?
The darkness conjured pictures of men,
who had no choice -
forcing their way through soil and rocks,
digging towards the future
that many would never see.

As we marched through the gloom,
in awe of the strength and grit
that echoed round that place,
the voices from the past came near.
They whispered low and soft, but clear,
"Even by fire we will not be defeated!"

Julie Collins

The Troubled Tunnel

This is the first train to pass through Summit Tunnel.
I sit by the window but I am uneasy.
Soon, only reflections of faces on glass, will be visible.

From the window I see dour Pennine hills
rising above stark, leafless branches of trees
surrounding Littleborough railway station.

A whistle is blown by the Station Master,
which sets in motion clanking pistons,
driving huge, iron wheels forward. We move with a lurch.

Familiar landscape chugs by me in my vantage position.
Glimpses of the canal with loaded, heavy barges and here,
as we approach the tunnel, I see Rock Nook Mill.

Whoosh! From light into darkness we are pitched.
Eerie candle lamps illuminate the coach,
and I'm very conscious of the rocking motion of the carriage.

Fear of this interminable darkness invades me,
I see a face, pale unnatural, staring in at me.
I hear a banging, clanging noise on the side of the train.

A vaporous breath flies by, a stream of white.
Is it steam from the train or the dying breath of a horse,
crushed by falling rocks during excavation of the tunnel?

Peering through the windows I can make out abandoned
shovels, old lanterns, tin pails, an ancient halter,
strewn alongside the track. Relics of manual tribulations.

Another face appears in the glass, bloodied, accusing.
It opens its mouth at me, a gaping black hole,
I cover my ears at that agonising, piercing scream.

And with a whoosh, we are out of that nightmare,
out of that darkness, out of that tunnel into the light,
released from the horror of Summit Tunnel's construction.

Glenis Meeks

Something's burning

On the eve of Yule, a train brimming with fuel, entered
the tunnel at Summit.
Then deep underground came an ominous sound, as a
wheel from the rail did plummet.
Next the brake system failed, and the train was derailed.
An inferno ensued, and later it proved 'twas a faulty
wheel bearing wot done it!

Chris Spankie

Fire in the Railway Tunnel

Scratch, scratch, scratch,
puny humans scratched at the earth.
Lucifer heard, raising his head,
swore at the humans disturbing his rest.
Took 41 souls for invading his kingdom,
cursing the angels who lived in the light.

Almost one hundred and fifty years later
his revenge on humans came to pass.
A defective axle derailed a fourth tanker,
this in its turn derailed all the rest.
A punctured tanker released petrol
and vapour. Crew took to their heels
to raise the alarm. Returning uncoupling,
they made safe the tankers, ensuring
security safe on the rails.

Fuel rich gases searched for the Oxygen
vapour reached shafts, cleaved to the air.
Pillars of fire with burning projectiles,
roared to the sky, instilling fear.
Lucifer laughed, watched with enjoyment,
as firemen, policemen fought to contain
the largest ever fire in tunnel construction.

Turning his back on such devastation
the Devil returned to his underground home
deep in the darkness he wanders alone.

Eileen Earnshaw

Beautiful feet

"He had beautiful feet" she said
seeing the form of her husband lying dead,
A victim of the tunnel....

The workers were busy
their tasks were set down.
Shovels and picks
were hitting the ground.

A train was approaching
the warning not sounded;
the men, unaware, so
their tools still pounded.

They should have stepped back
to refuge at the side.
All went unheeded
so all of them died....

"She has beautiful feet" she says
seeing the form of her first-born.
Fatherless,
a victim of the tunnel.

Dedicated to Auny Iris
Christine Longhurst

Into Darkness

(The Summit tunnel, Littleborough, was opened on Dec 9, 1840. The engineer, Barnard Dickenson, declared it would defy the rage of tempest, fire or wasting age.)

To defy the rage of tempest, fire or wasting age,
Barnard Dickenson, engineer,
mounts a platform to great acclamation
and with silver trowel lays
the fifteen millionth brick
as cannon fire in celebration,
to defy the rage of tempest, fire or wasting age.

To defy the rage of tempest, fire or wasting age
candlelight shines on glistening limbs
as moleskin grafters hack and dig.
In butty gangs, for five bob a day,
inching forward into darkness,
darkness filled with stench of sweat,
with smack of hammer, crack of pick.
Despite torrents of water and falls of rock
they blast and burrow into the mountain,
to defy the rage of tempest, fire or wasting age.

Chris O'Ryan

Summit or nadir?

Myopic, like moles they clawed the earth,
guided by only candles' light.
Was this the measure of their worth?
A tunneller's toil to be their plight?
Their aim to run a railway line
from Byron's County palatine.
Lancs to Yorks through a Pennine hill,
starting after Rock Nook Mill.
There laboured locals, once self-employed
as factory fodder, they're now deployed.
Clickety clack is the sound that they hear,
clickety clack of the looms weaving fear.
Fear of starvation, death and ill health,
whilst mill owners prosper flaunting their wealth.

Chris Spankie

The Pennine Ring

Raindrops filling moorland bogs,
dark peaty, stagnant water
seeping down wild rocky slopes,
through heath and cotton sedge.

Uneven, mossy outcrops,
sharp edges jutting out,
tiny glistening rivulets
slowly trickle their way down.

Water running into crags,
foamy, gushing streams
flooding paths and muddy tracks,
in rural Pennine valleys.

When the innovations came,
crews were out in force,
canals and reservoirs dug out -
The Pennines put to use.

Mill towns thrived in smog filled valleys
terraced rows built back-to-back,
housing workforce to produce
cotton-fibre khaki twills.

Canal boats on The Pennine Ring
used to transport goods,
ten times more efficient than
uneven packhorse routes.

Eventually the mills declined
around The Pennine Ring,
abandoned buildings derelict,
their structures caving in.

Few of cotton trade's remains
were salvaged from destruction;
The Pennine Ring now a natural link
of green wildlife corridors.

A never-ending waterflow
still tops up the canals -
nothing more reliable
than rainfall on the moors.

Sandra Buckley

The Summit Pound

The Summit Pound is empty'
drained by the heat.
Signs of drought everywhere
climate change in action

Lack of water exposing
dead cat, shoes and garbage,
rusty trollies abandoned.
The downside of human action

Don't people care?
Thoughtless, or vandalism?
Destroying wildlife, poisoning fish,
silent tears my only action.

Elizabeth White